HILLS VS. MOUNTAINS

KNOWING THE DIFFERENCE

GEOLOGY BOOKS FOR KIDS

Children's Earth Sciences Books

Our beautiful Earth is not all flat. The ground is higher in some places and lower in others. We call some high places *"Mountains"* and others *"Hills"*. What's the difference between them? Read on and find out!

Starry night over a mountain.

MOUNTAINS AND HILLS

It's harder than you think to know the difference between mountains and hills. For one thing, the local people might call the high place near them a *"Mountain"* while scientists might say, *"No, that's far too small. It's just a hill."* As you can imagine, the local people might not be happy hearing that!

Geologists are scientists who study land-forms. They generally say that the high place on dry land is a mountain if it is more than a thousand feet higher than the land around it. If the high place is shorter than that, it is probably a hill.

Geologists also say that mountains have steeper sides than hills. But both mountains and hills share this: you can generally tell when you are standing at the top of one, no matter what it is called, because you are higher up than anything nearby.

Gorgeous Landscape of Norway.

NAMES ARE IMPORTANT

Government bodies in the United Kingdom, Canada, and the United States used to have clear rules about how high a high place had to be for it to be a mountain. But since the 1970s government bodies have been paying more attention to what the local people say the high place is. If the local people call it a *"mountain"*, then that's how scientists refer to it, too.

Air view of Pakistan mountains along the way to Osaka.

Just to confuse things, there are other local names for high points of land, including *"butte"* and *"peak"*. Everybody agrees that peaks are tall mountains, but there is no clear rule about the height of buttes.

In 1995 there was even a movie about local people fighting to make the government call their local high place a mountain. The movie was set in Wales and was called *The Englishman That Went Up a Hill and Came Down a Mountain*. It is a good story about how important names of things are to people, but it is not clear that it is based on a true story.

In South Dakota there is a mountain range that rises almost 3,000 feet above the local area, and over 7,000 feet above sea level. But the Lakota Indians called these high areas *"paha sapa"*, which means *"the black hills"*. So if you look on a map you can see The Black Hills as the name of these mountains.

Tablelands in Newfoundland.

DECIDING WHICH IS WHICH

When you look at a high place and want to decide what to call it, the first thing is to find out what the local people call it. But if there are no local people around, here are some guidelines:

WHAT MAKES IT A HILL?

That high point of land is probably a hill if:

- It is sort of rounded, like a mound or a dome, rather than having a sharp point.

- It is a natural mound created by the action of the Earth, not by people piling up earth.

- It is like a *"bump"* in the surrounding landscape.

- Even if it stands out from the local landscape, it is not all that high.

- It may not have a name, or has several names depending on who you ask.

- It is pretty easy to climb. You don't need special equipment or to be an athlete to get to the top of it.

Rock formation near Acoma Pueblo, New Mexico.

WHAT MAKES IT A MOUNTAIN?

The high point of land is probably a mountain if:

- It has steeper sides and seems to rise higher from the surrounding area.

- There may be a lot of hills near a mountain, and the mountain will look sharper and rougher than the hills.

- It is far too big to be something humans made by piling up earth.

- It has a pointy top.

- It can be harder to climb. The sides may be steeper, and you have to travel further to get to the top.

Scenic landscape of Dolomite Alps
with forest and mountains.

COOL MOUNTAIN FACTS

THEY ARE OLD

It takes millions of years to make a mountain. Some mountains form because volcanoes erupt and throw out tons of rock, ash, and lava. The volcano erupts again and again over thousands of years, building up the land around it. The Hawaiian Islands are the very tips of huge volcanoes that sit on the bottom of the sea.

Read the Baby Professor book *What Happens Before and After Volcanoes Erupt?* to learn more about this kind of mountain.

Other mountains form because of movement of the Earth's crust. The crust is made of huge areas called *"tectonic plates"*. When these plates push into each other, very slowly, over millions of years, the surface of the Earth pushes up into mountains. The Himalayas in India, the highest mountain range in the world, formed this way-inch by inch, year by year.

THEY HAVE DIFFERENT SHAPES

Some mountains, like the Rockies in North America and the Himalayas, are sharp and rugged. Others are more gradual in shape. The less-rugged mountains, called *"Dome Mountains"*, form from volcanic action when the volcano keeps spewing out material over thousands of years, like a river of rock. The material, as it cools, builds up the land around. The Adirondack Mountains in the eastern United States are dome mountains.

Cloudy snow-capped rocky mountain peak.

THE HIGH HIMALAYAS

The Himalayan mountains include more than 30 of the tallest mountains on Earth. This includes the very tallest, Mount Everest. Its peak is over 29,000 feet above sea level.

THEY ARE OFTEN WILD

It is much easier to build towns, grow crops, raise animals, and travel on flat land or even hills than it is in mountains. So mountains are usually much wilder places. They are home to many types of animals that have been pushed out of lower land by human activity like farming.

Annapurna Mountain Range.

When there are wars or other troubles be-tween peoples, families and even whole tribes may move into the mountains to escape people who want to hurt them.

A WHOLE BUNCH OF MOUNTAINS

A string of mountains that are near each other and that were caused by the same natural events are called a mountain range. The Rocky Mountains in North America stretch from Canada in the north into Mexico in the south.

Evening view of Ama Dablam.

PLATEAUS AND FAULT BLOCKS

Some mountains look sort of tall and square, and are called Plateau mountains. They happened when two tectonic plates pressed into each other and part of one of the plates rose up without twisting or turning very much.

At other places on Earth, when tectonic plates press into each other, the rock crumples into huge, sharp-looking shapes. These are called Fault Block mountains.

Rock formations in monument valley.

A LOT OF MOUNTAINS!

Mountains cover about 20% of the Earth's dry land, and as much as 10% of the Earth's population live in the mountains.

MOUNTAINS IN THE WATER

There are more mountains in the ocean than there are on land! Some islands that rise only a few hundred feed above sea level are actually the very top part of huge mountains that reach down to the bottom of the sea.

Late autumn sunset on alpine pastures and mountains in Austria.

MOUNTAINS AND OUR ENVIRONMENT

About 80% of fresh water falls as snow or rain in mountains. Then, over time, it moves down toward sea level, feeding streams and rivers on its way. Without the flow of fresh water from the mountains, there would not be enough water for farming or for all the uses people need it for.

There is a narrower range of plant life in the mountains than there is at sea level. Like the animals, the plants have to be able to handle a rougher climate.

Zugspitze Mountain.

Green hills and cloudy sky view.

COOL FACTS ABOUT HILLS

And here are some fun things to know about hills:

THE S-SHAPED SLOPE

Lots of hills curve down for a short time at the top, and then curve back the other way as you move down toward the bottom. This makes what geologists call a *"convexo-concave"* profile.

WEARING AWAY

Hills have more gradual slopes because weather and erosion have worn them away. Many hills were once much higher, even mountains.

Hills wear away more quickly in warm, moist climates, as there is more water flowing and carrying away bits of the hill's material.

The solid rock of a hill, as it wears away, forms a layer of broken pieces called a regolith. The regolith slowly moves down the hill, but some-times a large part of the regolith can slide down the hill all at once in a landslide.

A MIX OF MATERIAL

While mountains are mainly rock with a thin skin of soil, hills can have a mix of rock and soil. Often this material was left by glaciers at the end of ice ages, as the glaciers retreated toward the poles or back into the mountains.

John Day Fossil Beds National Monument.

European Alps

THIS AMAZING EARTH

Now you know a bit about mountains and hills. There is much more to learn about the Earth! Read Baby Professor books like *Peeling the Earth Like an Onion, A Giant Shield,* and *Rocks and What We Know about Them* to learn even more!

Visit
BABY PROFESSOR
EDUCATION KIDS
www.BabyProfessorBooks.com
to download Free Baby Professor eBooks
and view our catalog of new and exciting
Children's Books